# Aboriginal

## ART & CULTURE

## Jane Bingham

**Raintree**

Chicago, Illinois

© 2005 Raintree
Published by Raintree, a division of Reed Elsevier, Inc.
Chicago, Illinois
Customer Service 888-363-4266
Visit our website at www.raintreelibrary.com

For information, address the publisher:
Raintree, 100 N. LaSalle, Suite 1200, Chicago, IL 60602

09 08 07 06 05
10 9 8 7 6 5 4 3 2 1

Produced for Raintree by White-Thomson Publishing Ltd.
Editorial: Kay Barnham, Nicole Irving, and Louise Galpine
Design: Simon Borrough and Ron Kamen
Illustrations: Tinstar Design
Picture Research: Elaine Fuoco-Lang
Production: Amanda Meaden

Originated by Ambassador Litho Ltd.
Printed and bound in Hong Kong, China by South China Printing Company

**Library of Congress Cataloging-in-Publication Data**
Bingham, Jane.
  Aboriginal art and culture / Jane Bingham.
    p. cm. -- (World art and culture)
  Includes bibliographical references and index.
  ISBN 1-4109-1106-3
  1. Art, Aboriginal Australian. 2. Aboriginal Australians--
Material culture. 3. Aboriginal Australian--Social life and customs.
I. Title. II. Series: World art & culture.
  GN666.B55 2005
  700′.89′9915--dc22
                        2004008074

**Acknowledgments**
The author and publisher would like to thank the following for permission to reproduce copyright material:
AKG p. 27; Australian Picture Library pp. 9, 19, 33, 35, 44; Bridgeman Art Library pp. 1, 14, 29 (Corbally Stourton Contemporary Art, London, UK), 15, 31 (Dreamtime Gallery, London), 36 (Horniman Museum, London, UK), 16 (Kakaku National Park, Australia), 43 (National Library of Australia, Canberra, Australia), 48, 51 (Private Collection); Corbis pp. 7, 23 (Corbally Stourton Contemporary Art, London, UK), 24, 49 (Araluen Arts Center), 17, 21, 42 (Charles & Josette Lenars), 28, 37 (John Van Hasselt), 5, 20, 25, 26, 39, 45, 46, 47 (Penny Tweedie), 41 (Will Burgess/Reuters); Harcourt pp. 11 (Bettmann), 13 (Corbis), 10 (Van Hasselt John/Corbis Sygma).

Cover photograph printed with kind permission of Bridgeman Art Library.

The publisher would like to thank Zoy Crizzle and Zane Ma Rhea for their assistance in the preparation of this book.

Every effort has been made to contact copyright holders of any material reproduced in this book. Any omissions will be rectified in subsequent printings if notice is given to the publisher.

Some words appear in bold, **like this.** You can find out what they mean by looking in the glossary.

# Contents

# Introduction

The Aboriginal people of Australia have lived on the vast continent for more than 40,000 years. For most of this time, they have survived by gathering food, hunting, fishing, and sometimes growing crops. Australian Aboriginals have a rich cultural life, creating paintings, sculptures, and carvings; telling stories; and performing dances and songs, all of which reflect their close relationship with the land and celebrate the power of their **ancestor spirits.**

## Changing lives

The Aboriginal way of life continued unchanged for thousands of years. However, in 1770 Captain James Cook arrived in Australia from Great Britain, and gradually British settlers took control of the land. While some Aboriginals put up a fierce fight, many were forced to retreat into the less **populated,** drier parts of the continent.

Today, many Aboriginal people live in towns and cities, while others live in **settlements,** mainly in the central desert regions or in the northern part of Australia. They belong to groups known as **societies,** such as the Anangu of central Australia and the Yolngu of the Northern Territory. Within these societies, they live in smaller family groups.

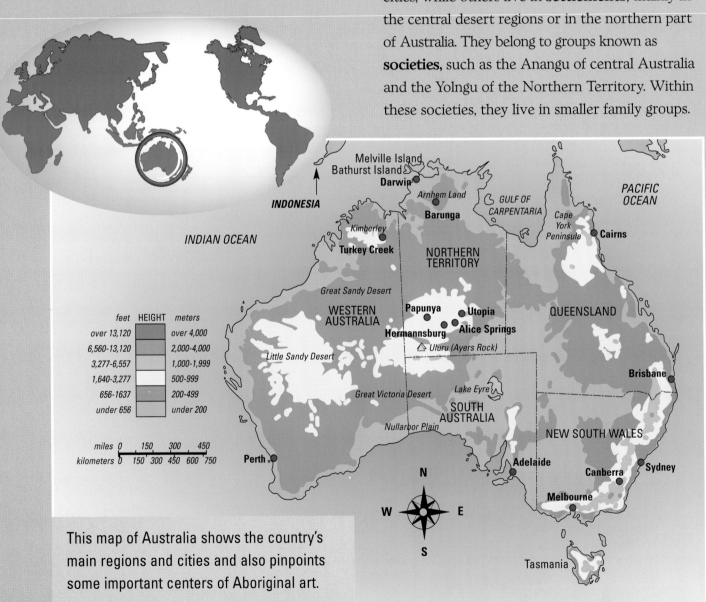

| feet | HEIGHT | meters |
|---|---|---|
| over 13,120 | | over 4,000 |
| 6,560-13,120 | | 2,000-4,000 |
| 3,277-6,557 | | 1,000-1,999 |
| 1,640-3,277 | | 500-999 |
| 656-1637 | | 200-499 |
| under 656 | | under 200 |

miles 0   150   300   450
kilometers 0   150  300  450  600  750

This map of Australia shows the country's main regions and cities and also pinpoints some important centers of Aboriginal art.

Aboriginal artists today paint traditional subjects but also introduce **motifs** of their own. This artist has painted areas of **crosshatched,** shimmering pattern on bark in the traditional Arnhem Land style.

## Aboriginal art today

Aboriginal people produce different types of art, depending on the traditions of their societies and also on the impact of Western culture in their area.

In the heavily populated south and southeast, little Aboriginal culture has remained, although the area still has a tradition of **engraving** wooden objects. In the sandy central regions, the people practice **ground art,** producing temporary sculptures made from earth and marking out large drawings on the ground. In the north and northeast of Australia, there are thriving traditions of bark painting, **rock painting,** sculpture, and basketwork. In the west and northwest, boab nut carvings and **emu** egg carvings are still produced.

As well as creating traditional works of art, Aboriginal artists in many parts of Australia experiment with new forms, materials, and media. However, experimental artists continue to draw on ancient traditions, fusing traditional imagery with new art forms, such as photography, computer imaging, and performance art.

## A sacred art

The Aboriginal people believe that the spirits of their ancestors wandered over Earth in a time known as the **Dreamtime,** creating the landscape and everything in it. The belief that all aspects of life were created by the ancestor spirits is expressed in everything the Aboriginal people make. From simple baskets to detailed paintings, their art celebrates the ancestor spirits and connects artists to their ancient past.

### ◇ Aboriginal or indigenous Australians

The word *aboriginal* comes from the Latin *ab origine,* meaning "from the beginning." It is used to describe the people who lived in a land first, before later settlers arrived. The original people of Australia are often known as Aboriginal people or Aboriginals, but it is now becoming much more common for them to call themselves **indigenous** Australians.

## A long history

There is evidence that people have lived in Australia for more than 40,000 years, although no one is certain how the first Australians came to be on the continent. Some experts believe that ancestors of the Aboriginal people traveled from Southeast Asia during the last **Ice Age** when water levels in the oceans were much lower than they are today. At that time, Asia and Australia were much larger than their present size, and a string of islands lay between the two vast continents. These early, island-hopping journeys may have continued until about 10,000 B.C.E., when the Ice Age ended and the melting ice caused sea levels to rise, cutting off Australia from the rest of the world.

Some Aboriginal paintings, songs, and stories include accounts of long ocean voyages undertaken by the **ancestor spirits,** and these stories of voyages may refer to the journeys of the earliest Australians to discover new land.

## Exploring the land

Over the course of thousands of years, the Aboriginal people made great journeys of exploration. This process happened extremely slowly, but by around 30,000 B.C.E., there is evidence that the Aboriginal people were established throughout the whole of Australia.

The great early journeys of exploration across Australia are remembered in Aboriginal art and culture as the **Dreamtime,** the time when the ancestor spirits traveled across the land, molding the country's features and creating its plants and animals. This very important period in the history of the Aboriginal people, when each **society** claimed its own territory, forms the central subject of Australian **indigenous** art.

## A changing land

Before the end of the Ice Age, Australia was covered in fertile plains with enormous lakes and lush forests. Huge prehistoric creatures roamed the land.

However, the landscape changed dramatically in about 10,000 B.C.E. as the climate became warmer. Lakes and rivers dried up and barren deserts appeared, while many creatures became extinct. The coastal floods and volcanic eruptions that also took place are recorded in Aboriginal stories.

### ◈ A great voyage

Some indigenous songs and stories describe a great voyage undertaken by the ancestor spirits to reach their homeland. In some stories, the spirits take on human form and in some they are animals. One story describes a canoe race between the ancestors of the koala, the starfish, and the whale. The starfish and the whale lose the race and have to spend the rest of their lives in the water, but the koala wins and reaches the land.

*c.* 40,000 B.C.E.: First evidence of Aboriginal people living in Australia.

*c.* 30,000 B.C.E.: Indigenous people have spread all over Australia.

*c.* 10,000 B.C.E.: Ice Age comes to an end. "Dynamic style" rock painting begins in Arnhem Land.

Many Aboriginal works of art record the great journeys of the ancestor spirits during the Dreamtime. This painting, entitled *Snake Dreaming* (1990), shows the Snake Ancestor's journey across the land. The spears and **boomerangs** on the left probably indicate where a hunt took place.

*c.* 7000 B.C.E.: "X-ray" style painting begins in Arnhem Land.

*c.* 6000 B.C.E.: "Guyon figures" are painted in northwest Australia.

*c.* 1500 B.C.E.: Wandjina painting begins in northwest Australia.

## An unchanging lifestyle

For thousands of years, the Aboriginal people followed the same way of life. They lived in small family groups. They hunted wild animals, caught fish, and gathered food from plants. Each group belonged to a larger **society.** All members of the society spoke the same language and lived in the same territory, known to Aboriginal people as a **country.** These areas could be very large, especially in the desert, where one society's territory might cover thousands of square miles.

Knowledge of a society's territory was passed down from one generation to the next through stories, songs, and ceremonies **commemorating** the **Dreamtime.** Within their territory, the family groups moved from place to place in search of food, setting up simple shelters wherever they went. When the Europeans arrived, there were more than 500 societies scattered throughout Australia, speaking at least 200 different languages.

## Visitors from Indonesia

In about 1650 C.E., fishers from the island of Macassar (present-day Sulawesi) in Indonesia began arriving on the northern coast of Australia in small sailing boats. Macassan fishermen returned each year to harvest sea slugs. They set up temporary villages along the coast of eastern Arnhem Land, spending several months and sometimes years there.

The Macassans continued to visit Australia for the next three centuries and developed good relationships with the **indigenous** people. The Aboriginals exchanged goods in return for objects such as metal axes and spearheads, and the Macassan culture had a significant impact on their art. Macassan objects such as knives, guns, anchors, and flags are represented in Aboriginal paintings. Local dances reflect the life and work of the Macassan people, and Macassan words occur in Aboriginal songs.

## Settlers from Britain

In 1770 Captain Cook arrived in Australia and claimed the eastern part of the country for the British king. At that time, jails in Great Britain were very crowded, and in 1788 the First Fleet reached Sydney, including six ships carrying **convicts** to settle in Australia. Many more British convict ships followed.

### ◈ An empty land?

Soon after the arrival of the First Fleet, British lawyers declared that Australia was *terra nullius,* meaning "empty land." The settlers claimed that this ruling gave them the right to seize any land they wanted. The *terra nullius* ruling was finally overturned in 1992 by the Australian High Court.

---

*c.* 1650: Macassan fishers start to visit Australia.

1770: Captain James Cook lands in Australia and claims it for Britain.

1788: The First Fleet arrives and sets up a **penal colony** in Sydney.

1901: Australia becomes a self-governing country.

Very soon, other settlers arrived from Europe and began seizing land, turning Australia into a **colony** governed by British officials. The colonists built towns and cities, while enormous stretches of land were covered by their farms.

Aboriginal rock paintings record the arrival of the Europeans with images of their boats and wagons, horses, cattle, and sheep. Unfortunately, there was little positive contact between the two cultures.

This rock painting shows a fishing boat dragging a large net. The vessel may have belonged to the Macassans or to Europeans who fished off the Australian coast.

1928: Massacre of members of the Warlpiri people—the last of many massacres.

1929: First major exhibition of Aboriginal art is held in Melbourne.

1967: Full citizens' rights are granted to the Aboriginal people.

1971: Western Desert Art Movement begins.

## Fighting for rights

In the 1930s groups of Aboriginals began to fight for their rights. It was a long struggle, but in 1967 the Australian government finally recognized the **indigenous** people as full citizens, with the same rights as all other Australians. This was a big step, but the indigenous people still felt that their rights to their land had not been recognized. In 1972 they set up the Aboriginal Tent Embassy, pitching their tents in front of **Parliament** House in Canberra.

Fights for land rights continued through the 20th century, gaining support from many white Australians. In the 1980s the Australian government passed laws protecting indigenous culture, and during the 1990s new laws were introduced that recognized the Aboriginals' right to land that had been continuously inhabited by their people.

## The fate of the Aboriginals

All over Australia, settlers from Europe drove the Aboriginal people from their land. Thousands died from European diseases such as smallpox, measles, and influenza, while the settlers' cattle and sheep destroyed many traditional water holes.

Some Aboriginals fought the settlers, killing cattle and sheep and burning crops. There were also brutal killings on both sides. Whole **societies** were wiped out and over a period of 150 years nearly 80 percent of the Aboriginal people were killed.

The new Australians set up **reservations** (known as reserves in Australia) where indigenous people could live. However, Aboriginals had no real rights. They had to gain permission from the white reservation manager to marry, to work, or even to receive a letter.

One of the ambassadors for the Aboriginal people prepares to sit in the famous Tent Embassy of 1972. The protest continues up to the present day, as indigenous people still camp outside Parliament House in Canberra, the Australian capital city.

1972: Aboriginal Tent Embassy is set up in Canberra.

1981: First major traveling exhibition of Aboriginal art is shown in four Australian cities.

1984: The National Aboriginal Art Award is established.

1985: Uluru (Ayers Rock), in the Northern Territory, is returned to its indigenous owners.

Aboriginal settlements are often in remote areas and have very few **amenities**.

## Aboriginal people today

Many Aboriginal people today live in towns or cities—especially in the south and southeast of Australia. But others live together in **settlements** in the more remote areas of the country, such as the central desert, the Kimberley Mountains in the northwest, northern Queensland, and Arnhem Land. Although most no longer live off the land, some Aboriginals try to continue their traditional way of life, singing songs, performing ceremonies, and creating paintings and sculptures.

### ◆ The Barunga Statement

In 1988 a group of Aboriginals presented a statement to the Australian Government at Barunga, in the Northern Territory. The statement called on the government to recognize the prior ownership rights of the Aboriginal people to certain areas of land. It was typed on a single sheet of paper and mounted on a large board made from bark, surrounded by painted designs. The designs, which showed the native creatures and features of their country, expressed the rights of the Aboriginal people just as clearly as their typewritten words.

**1992:** The Mabo case ruling recognizes that Australia was never a *terra nullius*.

**1993:** The Native Title Act is passed, recognizing Aboriginal land rights.

**1997:** Three Aboriginal women artists represent Australia at the Venice Biennale Art Festival.

**2000:** Aboriginal people take part in Corroboree 2000 as part of National Reconciliation Week.

# Beliefs and Traditions

The Aboriginal people believe that the **ancestor spirits** created everything in the world during the **Dreamtime,** and these beliefs are central to all forms of their art. Songs, dances, and paintings record events that happened in the Dreamtime. Even functional objects, such as spears or baskets, are filled with religious meaning. They are believed to have been created by the ancestor spirits.

## Ancestor spirits

In the songs, dances, and stories of the **indigenous** people, the ancestor spirits take many different forms. Sometimes they are humans, but often they are creatures, such as kangaroos or crocodiles, or even physical features, such as rocks or trees. According to Aboriginal beliefs, ancestor spirits often changed shape—swimming like fish, jumping like kangaroos, singing songs like humans, and even transforming themselves into rocks or trees.

## Special spirits

Each region and **society** has its own ancestor spirits, but some of the best known figures are the Sky Heroes of southern Australia, the Great Earth Mother and the Rainbow Serpent of the Northern Territory, and the Seagull Hero of Western Australia.

In traditional Aboriginal society, each individual is watched over by his or her own particular spirit. From the time of conception, the person is linked to this spirit, and this affects the range of subjects he or she can show in his or her art.

## The Dreamtime

According to Aboriginal beliefs, the Dreamtime was a period when the ancestor spirits walked all over, creating everything. The spirits created the landscape, the sun and stars, and the seasons and weather. They also created humans, animals, and plants.

During the Dreamtime, the spirits went on long journeys, hunted, and fought, and many of the events from their lives are recorded as features in the landscape. These permanent reminders of events in the Dreamtime have become **sacred sites** for the Aboriginal people.

## ◈ The creation of Uluru

The massive rock formation of Uluru (called Ayers Rock by the European settlers) is a sacred Aboriginal site, and many traditional stories describe its creation in the Dreamtime. One of the most common stories claims that Uluru was the camp of the Carpet Snake Spirits who lived there for thousands of years before they were turned into stone. According to the stories, the spirits fought a great battle to defend their camp, spilling large quantities of blood. This legend explains why the rock turns blood-red at sunset.

At sunrise and sunset, the sacred rock of Uluru (Ayers Rock) in the Northern Territory is a dramatic sight.

## Dreaming tracks

According to Aboriginal beliefs, the **ancestor spirits** undertook astonishing journeys across the continent of Australia, creating a pattern of **dreaming tracks** that crisscrossed the landscape in a vast maze. Along the way, the spirits performed actions that molded and formed the land into the shapes that exist today.

## Tracing the tracks

The great journeys of the ancestor spirits have been remembered for generations in ceremonies that can last for days, or even weeks. In these ceremonies, groups of **indigenous** people follow a track, stopping to perform lengthy cycles of songs at particular places where a spirit rested in a cave or created a boulder, lake, or water hole. The stopping points may also mark places where an ancestor paused to create a particular animal or plant. Here, ceremonies are held that are designed to release the ancestor's life-giving power and to make sure that the animal or plant will continue to flourish.

## Stories to live by

As well as creating everything on Earth, the ancestor spirits also taught the Aboriginal people how to live their lives. Through their many adventures, the spirits set up patterns for every aspect of life—hunting, cooking, marrying, and raising children. Traditional stories about the spirits are told by the **elders** of a **society** in order to teach the younger generation guidelines for living.

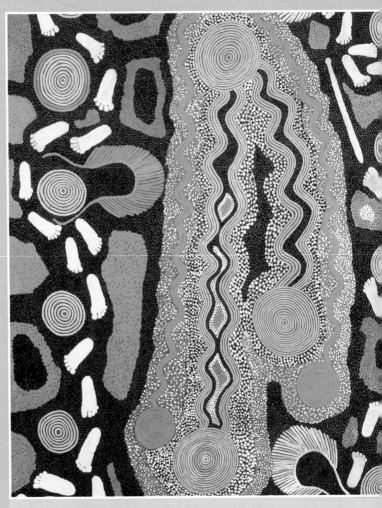

In this painting from 1975, the artist Anatjari Tjakamarra uses a set of footprints to mark out a dreaming track. The simplified heads, surrounded by a shock of hair, represent mischievous spirits.

## Mapping the tracks

As well as tracing the tracks in songs, dances, and ceremonies, Aboriginal people also mark out parts of a dreaming track by drawing patterns on the ground, or by making sculptures that act as markers for important events along the track.

Sometimes a dreaming track is drawn as a kind of map. These maps"of the tracks can be painted on bark or canvas or marked out on the ground. They often include landscape features or animals and plants that appear on the journey.

Many paintings relate the adventures of the ancestor spirits. Here, the Rainbow Serpent Ancestor has a meeting with another ancestor— possibly the Koala.

## ◈ Secret knowledge

The stories and ceremonies of the dreaming tracks are passed from generation to generation within a society and are very rarely revealed to outsiders. This means that any interpretation of the art of the tracks can never be complete. A few Aboriginal artists choose to explain some features of their art. However, artists are careful never to give away the entire meaning of a work of art.

# Rock Art

The **engravings** and paintings found on rock shelters are the oldest surviving form of Aboriginal art. The earliest known rock engravings date from around 30,000 B.C.E., while paintings have been found from around 20,000 B.C.E. However, experts believe that **rock painting** began much earlier than this. Surviving fragments of painted rock suggest that **indigenous** people began to decorate their landscape from the earliest times.

## Rock engravings

Some of the earliest markings on rock come from Koonalda Cave in the Nullarbor Plain of southern Australia. Here, the soft cave walls have been marked with meandering lines that look like spaghetti noodles.

Other early engravings show circles and lines and scattered animal footprints. The largest collection of carved geometric designs has been found in the deserts of southern Australia. But geometric carvings survive in sites all over Australia and also on the island of Tasmania.

## Early rock paintings

The earliest surviving rock paintings in Australia date from around 20,000 B.C.E. and show hand **stencils**, footprints, and animal forms, usually painted in red **ocher.** These simple, early designs are probably intended to show where an **ancestor spirit** passed by. However, by around 10,000 B.C.E. paintings on rocks had become much more sophisticated. As well as showing animals, they depict human figures engaged in a range of activities.

Two major groups of early paintings have been found in Australia. In Arnhem Land in northern Australia, a series of scenes in the dynamic style were painted from about 10,000 to 6000 B.C.E. Another set of paintings known as the Bradshaw or Guyon figures that date from about 6000 B.C.E. have been discovered in the Kimberley region, in northwest Australia.

These hand stencils found in the Kakadu National Park, Arnhem Land, may be about 20,000 years old.

16

## Dynamic style paintings

The dynamic style paintings of Arnhem Land were given their name because of their lively figures, which appear to be racing over the surface of the rocks. They were painted around the end of the last **Ice Age,** when sea levels were beginning to rise. The paintings show a range of land animals as well as ocean and river creatures.

Usually painted in red ocher, the dynamic style figures are tall, spindly, and often finely detailed. Many wear elaborate headdresses and carry weapons or fans. They are often shown in vigorous movement—hunting, fighting, or taking part in **rituals.** Depictions of fights in the paintings may indicate the growing competition for land at this time.

In the final phases of the dynamic style, about 3,000 years ago, the painted figures of Arnhem Land became less elegant and sticklike. Figures were drawn more simply and had rounded bodies and swollen-looking limbs.

These rock paintings from Arnhem Land are in the dynamic style. The elongated figures run energetically across the rock face, holding spears and fans.

### ◈ Natural pigments

Aboriginal artists have used the same natural **pigments** for thousands of years. Red and yellow ocher (earth colors) are made from ground-up rock. White is made from pipe clay, while black is produced from charcoal. The pigments are ground into a fine powder and mixed with a **binder,** such as the sap from an orchid plant, that holds the mixture together.

## Guyon figures

At about the same time as artists in Arnhem Land were producing their dynamic style paintings, another set of rock paintings were being created in the Kimberley region, in northwest Australia. The Guyon figures are painted in red **ocher.** They are elongated and elegant, with long limbs. But instead of being involved in dynamic action, they appear to be floating or dancing in a trancelike state. They also have weapons or **ceremonial objects.** The figures were first named after the explorer Joseph Bradshaw, who described them in the 1890s. However, senior leaders of the Ngarinyin people, in whose **country** the paintings are found, have asked that they be called by their Aboriginal name, Guyon.

## Wandjina paintings

Another group of paintings found in the Kimberley region are the Wandjina images. However, they are very different from the Guyon figures. The Wandjina tradition dates from about 1500 B.C.E. These paintings depict ancestor spirits known as Wandjina who emerged from the sea and the sky but were later absorbed into the rocks.

The Wandjina are semihuman figures, up to 23 feet (7 meters) tall, with circular heads, large, owl-like eyes, a drop-shaped nose, and no mouth. They often have ovals below their necks, representing either chest ornaments or their breastbones. The figures are outlined against white backgrounds and usually painted in black and white.

## A continuous tradition

For centuries, the painted Wandjina figures have been continually renewed. The Aboriginal people

## George Grey and the Wandjina

In the 1830s a British explorer named Sir George Grey discovered some Wandjina paintings. However, he thought the paintings were much too skillful to have been painted by Aboriginal artists. He came to the completely inaccurate conclusion that the Wandjina artists must have been taught or influenced by visitors from another culture.

of the western Kimberley region believe that the Wandjina spirits look after their crops, while certain Wandjina sites are connected with the conception of children. In order to make sure that their crops are watered and that they continue to give birth to children, the Aboriginal people take care of the Wandjina spirits, constantly repainting their images on rock shelters and caves. Local people also believe that they need to respect the paintings in order to avoid upsetting the Wandjina spirits and bringing punishments such as floods and thunderstorms.

The tradition of painting Wandjina figures continues today. Painters depict the figures on bark as well as rocks, while some contemporary indigenous artists have incorporated Wandjina images into their paintings on canvas.

## Wuruluwurulu paintings

There is a third tradition of rock painting in the Kimberley region. Wuruluwurulu figures are mischievous tricksters and sorcerers. These small, red ocher figures often appear on their own, but are also shown cutting across the painted Wandjina spirits, as if challenging their power.

This group of Wandjina heads from the Kimberley region is painted on the wall of a rock shelter. The painted heads have the characteristic owl-like eyes of the Wandjina spirits.

These X-ray paintings may date back to about 7000 B.C.E. They show the bones and organs of men and creatures in a highly patterned, **stylized** manner.

## X-ray paintings

Around 9,000 years ago a new style of rock painting began to appear in Arnhem Land. These paintings depicted animals and humans as though their bodies were transparent, revealing their internal organs and bones. The tradition of so-called X-ray painting on rocks has continued in northern Australia up to the present day, while a similar X-ray style is also used in bark paintings and body decoration.

The precise significance of the X-ray style cannot be understood by non-Aboriginal people. However, detailed X-ray images of fish, birds, and animals, such as kangaroos and turtles, were probably connected with hunting rituals.

## Records on rocks

Engravings and paintings on rocks provide a valuable record of major events in the history of the Aboriginal people. Rock paintings in Arnhem Land show the simple sailing boats of the Macassan fishermen who visited the coast every year from around 1650 to 1907. The arrival of the Europeans, from the 1770s onward, is recorded in paintings and carvings all over Australia. A set of fine engravings on rocks in the Hawkesbury region of Sydney shows the arrival of the First Fleet of British settlers. Carved outlines of wagons on rocks along the Hodgson River, in northern Australia, record the progress of the early cattle ranchers.

In western Arnhem Land, X-ray style paintings show many aspects of **colonial** life, including boats and barges, ranchers with horses and buffalo, and police officers and soldiers armed with guns. Some rock paintings even depict the military and civilian airplanes that were based in the northern city of Darwin in the early years of the 20th century.

A group of mischievous Mimi spirits chase across these rocks in Arnhem Land.

## Mimi figures

Mimis are tall, sticklike figures that appear in rock paintings of all ages in Arnhem Land. Like the Wuruluwurulu figures of the Kimberley region, they represent mischievous trickster spirits. Mimis are usually shown dancing. They often wear feathers in their hair and carry arrows and a **dilly bag.** Artists painting on bark sometimes show Mimi stick figures drawing their inspiration from the Mimis in rock art.

### ◈ Sacred colors

According to traditional Aboriginal beliefs, each color used in their paintings has a special significance: red symbolizes the blood shed by Marindi, the **Dingo** spirit; pipe-clay white was smeared over the body of Wirroowaa of the Lachlan River when he summoned the spirits to help his people; yellow **ocher** is the sacred color of the Yirritja people of northeastern Arnhem Land; and black represents the charcoal left from the campfires lit by the ancestors during the **Dreamtime.**

# Ground Art

Drawing on the ground and making sculptures from earth or stones are very important aspects of Aboriginal art. These art forms are part of the sacred activity of marking out the **dreaming tracks,** and are often combined with storytelling, singing, and dancing. They are also a valuable form of communication, teaching members of a **society** about the tracks in their **country.**

Aboriginal **ground art** can be temporary or permanent. Some arrangements of stones have stayed in place for thousands of years. Sometimes ground art is created before a ceremony to make a sacred space in which the ceremony can take place. However, the act of marking the ground can also be a part of the ceremony.

## Sand drawings

The **indigenous** people of central Australia have been drawing patterns in the desert for thousands of years. Although these drawings are temporary, they are part of a continuous tradition. The patterns are taught to each new generation of a society. Often, sand drawings trace the journeys and adventures of **ancestor spirits.** The drawings usually feature large geometrical patterns made up of circles, lines, and U-shapes, but may include smaller **motifs,** such as animal prints.

Sometimes a **ceremonial ground** is marked out, or a whole structure, such as a home for an ancestor, is built from sand. These structures are later used in ceremonies that reenact events from the ancestor's life.

## Making patterns and prints

Each central Australian society has its own set of patterns that are marked out in the sand with a stick, or using fingers and thumbs. Some of these patterns can only be understood by society members, but others are easier to recognize. A snake is represented by a wavy line, while a dog's paw and an **emu's** foot are easily recognized. Humans are often represented by simple footprints.

## Ground sculptures

Sculptures on the ground are made from rocks, sand, and earth, and they can incorporate complex constructions of branches, sticks, and string. They mark special places along a dreaming track—perhaps a place where a spirit stopped to rest or to create a creature.

Ground sculptures can still be seen in many parts of central Australia, where they are much more common than wooden sculptures. They probably originally occurred throughout Australia.

##  Many meanings

The shapes and symbols that appear in sand drawings and other forms of Aboriginal art can have many different meanings, depending on the story that is being told. For example, some of the many meanings of the U-shaped sign are a sitting man, a **boomerang,** and a windbreak.

The ancient traditions of drawing on sand are continued in the large-scale paintings of the Western Desert artists. Here, artist Clifford Possum Tjapaltijarri makes the same marks on his canvas as his ancestors made in the sand.

# Painting

Aboriginal artists produce many different types of paintings. They paint on rocks, shields, sculptures, musical instruments, and baskets. They also paint their bodies. Artists in northern Australia create paintings on panels made from bark, while many Aboriginal artists today choose to paint on canvas. This chapter concentrates on paintings on bark and canvas, but often the same styles and **motifs** are used in many different forms of painting.

## Sacred subjects

Some bark paintings showing sacred subjects play an important part in **rituals** and ceremonies. These panels may show **ancestor spirits,** legends from the **Dreamtime,** or maps of the land.

In eastern Arnhem Land, paintings are kept in special storehouses and shown to young members of the **society** at **initiation ceremonies** in order to teach them the secrets of their society. In western Arnhem Land, bark paintings are used as illustrations of sacred legends and stand in rows on the **ceremonial grounds.**

## Bark paintings

Bark paintings are mainly found in Arnhem Land, in northern Australia. They were originally painted on the inside walls of bark shelters, but since the 19th century few shelters have been built. Today, bark paintings are produced as individual panels, but they are still sometimes used to decorate homes.

Bark panels found in homes usually show images from everyday life. These paintings show animals such as kangaroos, birds, fish, and reptiles in the surrounding country. They may also show scenes of hunting, fishing, and gathering food.

Some bark paintings tell a complete narrative, like this story of a hunt.

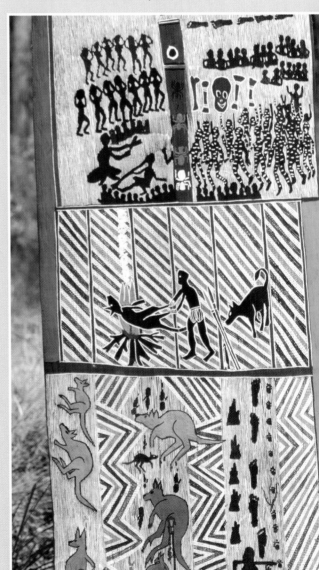

### Painting on bark

The Aboriginal people create bark panels by stripping a sheet of bark off the stringy-bark tree (a type of **eucalyptus**). The sheet is then flattened over a fire. Traditionally, painters applied their **pigments** to the bark using brushes made from chewed plant **fibers** or from strands of hair. Today, some painters use ordinary paintbrushes, although they still use natural pigments on bark.

An Arnhem Land artist carefully fills in the areas of crosshatching in his painting of an octopus ancestor.

## Special effects

Many of the bark paintings of eastern and central Arnhem Land include large areas of **crosshatched** patterns. The paintings are created by first covering the ground with a single color wash (usually red **ocher**), then sketching in the figures in yellow or black. After this, areas of the painting are filled with crosshatched lines of two different colors using a fine brush. Finally, the designs are given a second outline in white. The total effect is intended to reflect the power of the ancestor spirits.

## Special subjects

The range of subjects that an **indigenous** artist can show in a painting (or in any other form of art) is determined by that artist's **society.** Members of one group may depict the Great Earth Mother, while artists from another group may show the Seagull Hero Ancestor. It is strictly forbidden for an Aboriginal artist to show an ancestor or a myth that is associated with a different society.

## Painting for a wider public

Around the beginning of the 20th century, some Europeans began to take an interest in indigenous art and, in particular, paintings on bark. They encouraged artists in Arnhem Land to paint bark panels that could be exhibited in galleries. Gradually some artists began to create pictures to be displayed and sold. However, they were still very careful only to paint the subjects permitted by their society.

Paintings produced for public display from the mid-20th century onward included story paintings that related a complete Aboriginal legend in many scenes. Another popular type of bark painting is the clan painting. Clan paintings are large-scale cooperative works. They are created by the members of several family groups who all work together to produce a painting that combines a range of designs and stories.

## Board paintings

Artists in Turkey Creek, a **settlement** in northwest Australia, paint traditional designs on rectangular plywood boards, rather than bark panels. These painted boards, which are carried by dancers in ceremonies, are simple but dramatic. Many of them show black shapes of animals and plants surrounded by a border of white dots. The striking compositions of the Turkey Creek artists provided the inspiration for Rover Thomas, one of Australia's best known indigenous artists.

 **Rover Thomas**

The indigenous artist Rover Thomas (1926–1998) worked in cattle stations in the north of Western Australia, but at the age of 55 he settled in Turkey Creek and began to paint. His paintings often feature the animals and plants of the area, and many of them illustrate the story of a local old woman. The story was first revealed to him in a dream.

Thomas created a unique style that combined traditional techniques, such as the drawing of outlines with dotted lines, with confident brushwork. His bold, semiabstract compositions in traditional **ocher** colors appeal to a wide audience. Thomas was one of the first Australian artists to exhibit his work in international exhibitions.

Only an artist whose tribe is associated with the Rainbow Serpent is allowed to paint that spirit's image. Below, Aboriginal artist Pete Maralwonga displays his bark painting.

## Western Desert art

During the 1970s, a group of artists from Papunya —an Aboriginal **settlement** in the west of the central desert region—created a new kind of art. They showed traditional subjects using **acrylic paint** on canvas. For thousands of years, **indigenous** people in the central desert had been making **ground art** and painting on bodies and **ceremonial objects,** but they had never created large-scale paintings before. This new kind of painting became known as Western Desert art.

## Maps of the land?

Most Western Desert paintings show **Dreamtime** journeys. They include tracks and landscape features and have been compared to maps or aerial photographs. However, the paintings cannot be read like a conventional European map. Different parts of the track are made longer or shorter, according to how important they are, and landscape features, such as lakes or trees, are not shown in proportion to each other. The paintings usually feature a detailed exploration of a particular sacred area, while other stretches of the journey are just sketched in.

## Geoffrey Bardon and the Papunya School

The Western Desert Art Movement began in 1971, when Geoffrey Bardon, a teacher at the Papunya school, encouraged some of the settlement **elders** to paint some murals on the school walls. The first designs were painted by two groundskeepers at the school, but soon more people became involved.

Once the murals were finished, the artists wanted to continue painting, so Bardon provided them with boards and paint. Some of the paintings were sold to cover the costs of materials. The paintings became popular, first throughout the region and then across the whole country.

Papunya paintings are now exhibited and sold throughout Australia.

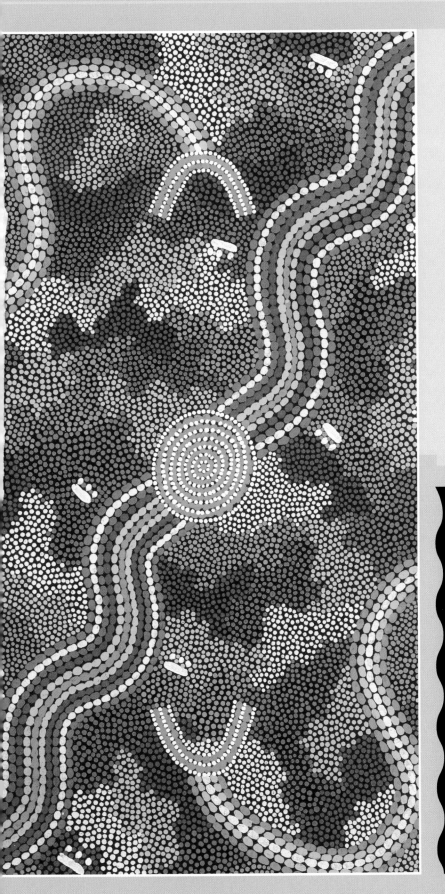

## The Tjapaltjarri brothers

Two of the most famous Western Desert artists are Clifford Possum Tjapaltjarri and his brother Tim Leura Tjapaltjarri. The Tjapaltjarri brothers produce images of the **dreaming tracks** that also feature symbolic humans and animals. Painting on huge canvases with a range of muted colors, the brothers have developed a technique of dotting their paint to create a shimmering effect.

*Dingo* Dreaming was painted by Clifford Possum Tjapaltjarri in 1990 and features the paw prints of a dingo.

### ◈ The circle and the line

Many Western Desert paintings feature circles and lines. These basic geometric elements, which also appear in sand drawings and rock **engravings,** can have many meanings. However, one of the clearest meanings is that a line represents a journey, while a circle is a stopping place. By creating an interconnected pattern of lines and circles, the artist is making a map of a Dreamtime journey and the incidents that took place along the way.

## Ginger Riley Munduwalawala

Ginger Riley Munduwalawala (1937–2002) came from the region around the Gulf of Carpentaria in northern Australia. He learned traditional methods of painting, working only with **ocher** colors until he reached the age of 50. Then, in 1987, he attended a painting class and began to work with acrylics. Munduwalawala's vivid paintings show his native river landscape dominated by the spirits of the Sea Eagle and the Serpent Creator. They are painted in brilliant reds, blues, and greens, but also include some ocher colors and elements of traditional local designs, such as patterns of lines and dots.

## Paintings from Utopia

By the 1980s artists from several communities in central Australia were following the lead of the Papunya painters, and they each created new styles. The **indigenous** community in Utopia already had a tradition of creating designs using the **batik** printing technique, but in the late 1980s women batik artists began to produce paintings instead. The early Utopia paintings tell traditional stories and feature the same repeated floral motifs that are used in the batiks. However, later individual artists developed their own styles.

## The Yuendumu cooperative

In the early 1980s, a group of artists belonging to the Yuendumu people in central Australia formed a **cooperative** to exhibit and sell their work. Like the Papunya artists, the Yuendumu artists painted in acrylics on canvas. Some members of the cooperative produced individual works of art, but most of the time many artists worked together on a single canvas.

By the 1990s, the Yuendumu cooperative was making large-scale paintings that were created by many members of their community. These gigantic works show events from the **Dreamtime** and are intended as part of the community's education. Each painting concentrates on a different **sacred site.** The artists begin with a visit to that site, where they sing the traditional songs. Young and old artists work together on the paintings. These paintings are seen as a valuable way of passing on knowledge of places, designs, and songs to the next generation.

## Emily Kame Kngwarreye

One of the most famous Utopian painters is Emily Kame Kngwarreye (c. 1910–1996), who only began painting in her late seventies. Her first paintings had an underlying structure of geometric plants and animals that she painted over with lines of dots. She later abandoned the underlying images and concentrated on the surface forms, creating flowing patterns using dots of different colors and sizes. Kngwarreye's final works are stark, two-color paintings, based on body painting designs.

In *My Country* (acrylic on canvas), Emily Kame Kngwarreye blurs her characteristic lines of dots to create an abstract effect similar to woven cloth.

# Sculpture and Carving

Sculptures in wood were probably once created in many parts of Australia, but now only scattered examples can be found. Some of the most dramatic sculptures are made on Bathurst and Melville Islands, off the northern coast of Australia. These islands were originally part of the mainland. Other striking examples survive in Arnhem Land, in northern Australia. Smaller-scale carvings are made in Cape York Peninsula in northern Queensland, and there is also evidence of a tradition of creating *toas,* or marker posts, in the Lake Eyre region of central Australia.

Tiwi people believe that a grave post represents the spirit of the dead person. The posts are carved in a **stylized** human shape and their decorations are similar in style to Tiwi body paintings. Designs often represent the **ancestor spirits** of a particular society.

This carved and painted kangaroo is in the tradition of the Cape York sculptures.

## Tiwi grave posts

The Tiwi people of Bathurst and Melville islands hold dramatic funeral ceremonies to mark the death of important men or women in their **society**. At the climax of these ceremonies, large carved and painted posts called Pukumani poles are placed around the grave as a final gift to the dead person and as a lasting **memorial.**

Tiwi artists prepare for the task of making a grave post by first finding a suitable hardwood tree and then meditating on the story for its carved and painted designs. However, carving must be completed quickly after a tree is chopped down before the wood begins to harden. Once the carving is done, the posts are rolled through a fire to dry the timber and prevent it from cracking. Then the posts are painted with traditional designs, and artists usually add some patterns of their own.

## Cape York sculptures

On the Cape York Peninsula in northern Queensland, the **indigenous** people carve small-scale wooden sculptures to be used in funerals and other ceremonies. The sculptures are painted in **ocher** colors and sometimes have details made from beeswax, feathers, horsehair, or leather.

The carvings may show an ancestor spirit, such as the Seagull Hero, or an object associated with a spirit, such as a digging stick, a canoe, or a paddle. Other sculptures illustrate events from the spirits' lives. A powerful carving by Jackson Woolla shows the terrible fate of a boy who was punished by the spirits for entering a forbidden place. He was made unable to walk again.

## Toas of Lake Eyre

Between 1888 and 1906, Pastor Johann Reuther, a Christian missionary in the Lake Eyre region of Central Australia, made a collection of painted *toas*. These small sculptures, which range in length from 6 to 22 inches (15 to 57 centimeters), consist of a pointed wooden peg with a knob made from gypsum (a type of natural plaster). The wooden base and knob are usually painted with **ocher,** and their designs include bands of color and dots. Sometimes other materials are attached to the knob such as bone, shell, wood, hair, or feathers.

The *toas* appear to have had a range of different uses. Some of them were probably used to mark an important place. For example, a *toa* of a pelican's head was probably used to identify Lake Tampangaraterkanani, which means "the lake where the pelicans stand." Other *toas* may have **commemorated** a special event on an **ancestor spirit's** journey. A carved foot may show where an ancestor stopped to rest, while a *toa* with a bone attached to it may represent a place where one of the ancestor's followers died.

Many experts believe that some of the *toas* in Pastor Reuther's collection may have been created by the **indigenous** people specifically for him. However, the Lake Eyre *toas* are probably all examples of an ancient tradition of using way markers to indicate important places on a **dreaming track.**

## Hollow log coffins

One of the ancient **rituals** still carried out by the people of central and eastern Arnhem Land is the Hollow Log Coffin or Bone Coffin ceremony. This involves the burying of a person's bones in a second burial ceremony some time after they have died.

In the first stage of the Bone Coffin ceremony, a suitable log is found that has already been hollowed out by **termites.** This log is taken to a special camp, where it is cleaned and painted with traditional designs while people perform songs and dances. The bones of the dead are also cleaned and painted with red ocher before being placed in the log.

When the series of songs and dances has been completed, dancers carry the log to the main public camp, where it is left standing upright. The Aboriginal people see the upright hollow log coffins as a forest containing the spirits of the dead.

## Boab nuts and emu eggs

Indigenous Australians believe that decorating objects with traditional patterns and stories helps to fill these objects with the powers of the ancestor spirits. The people of the Kimberley region in Western Australia have a long tradition of carving boab nuts (shown on the right). The dark-colored nuts are carved to reveal the lighter wood beneath. Traditionally, carvers showed

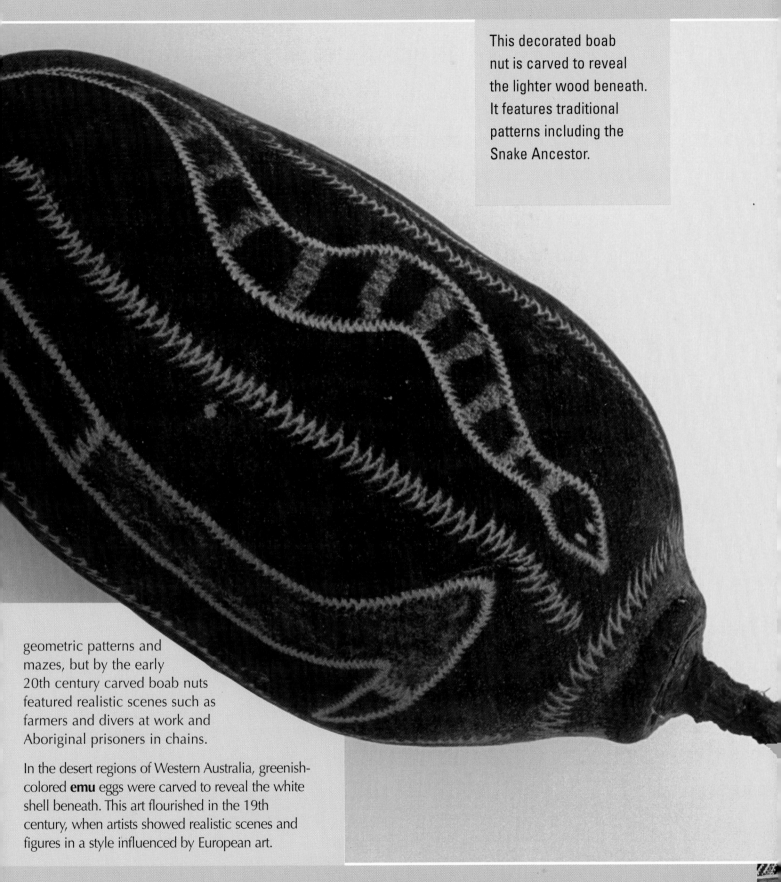

This decorated boab nut is carved to reveal the lighter wood beneath. It features traditional patterns including the Snake Ancestor.

geometric patterns and mazes, but by the early 20th century carved boab nuts featured realistic scenes such as farmers and divers at work and Aboriginal prisoners in chains.

In the desert regions of Western Australia, greenish-colored **emu** eggs were carved to reveal the white shell beneath. This art flourished in the 19th century, when artists showed realistic scenes and figures in a style influenced by European art.

# Weapons and Shields

Weapons and shields once played a vital part in the lives of the Aboriginal people, and there is still a thriving practice of making decorated shields, spear throwers, and **boomerangs.**

## Boomerangs

The boomerang is an Aboriginal invention that can be used as a weapon for hunting or fighting, a tool for cutting or digging, or as a **percussion instrument** for dances and songs. Some **indigenous** groups also hold events in which contestants compete to see how far they can throw the boomerang.

The light, but strong, returning boomerang was originally used for hunting water birds. It is mainly made in southeast and southwest Australia. The heavy, hooked boomerang (sometimes known as a **boomerang club**), which is used for hunting and killing larger animals, is found in most regions of the country. Boomerangs can be decorated with engraved carvings or with **pokerwork.** Recently, the boomerang has become a popular symbol in contemporary Aboriginal paintings.

## Spear throwers

The people of the central desert regions make spear throwers that allow them to throw their long, wooden spears distances of more than 300 feet (90 meters). The spear thrower consists of a flat, oval, wooden holder to which a kangaroo's claw or a wild dog's tooth is attached by a strong string made of gut. The spear rests on the wooden holder and its end is slotted into the tooth or claw. The spear is drawn back and then released, allowing it to travel very fast and accurately.

## Shields

The indigenous people of New South Wales and Victoria create wooden shields covered with elaborate carvings. Skilled carvers decorate the surface of the shields with deeply engraved geometric forms that are filled with **ocher.** Designs often consist of flowing parallel lines and sometimes also feature the outlines of animals.

A different type of decoration is found on the shields of the rain forest people of northern Queensland. These curved shields, made from the roots of fig trees, are painted with bold patterns that at first sight appear to be purely abstract. In fact, these patterns represent a range of creatures.

Queensland shields are decorated with semiabstract patterns that provide good camouflage in the rain forest.

These brightly painted boomerangs, made for the tourist market, are painted with symbols often found in Western Desert art.

## ◈ Patterns from shields

The Queensland ceramic artist Thancoupie decorates her pots with traditional animal patterns found on the shields of the region. The circular form of her pots is copied from the clay balls that were traditionally used as containers for ocher **pigments.**

# Body Art

Early Aboriginal **rock paintings** show people wearing a range of body art. In these paintings, hunters have painted bodies and wear nose pins, necklaces, pendants, and tasseled armbands. Dancers performing ceremonies wear elaborate headdresses that are sometimes decorated with feathers, pins, tassels, and strings. Today, most **indigenous** people wear Western clothing, but some still wear traditional ornaments and body paint for special ceremonies, such as initiations and funerals.

## Ornaments and adornments

Some body adornments, such as pendants or nose pins, may be worn every day, and these often indicate the **society** to which a person belongs. For example, the members of one group may wear a pendant made from a certain animal's teeth, while people from another group may wear a shell chest ornament. Other ornaments, such as feathered dancing belts, headdresses, or **mourning** armbands, are usually only worn for special occasions.

Sometimes an ornament shows a person's **status.** Aboriginal boys are often presented with a weapon belt when they reach **puberty,** and some southeastern Aboriginal women wear a ceremonial apron made from **emu** feathers. It is discarded after the birth of their first child.

## Natural materials

Body ornaments can be made from a wide range of materials. The Tiwi people of the Bathurst and Melville islands make armlets from bark and feathers and carve wooden pendants that are then decorated with seeds set in beeswax. The people of the Kimberley region in northwest Australia produce **engraved** pearl shell ornaments that are highly prized because of their shimmering surfaces. The Diyari people of the central desert region make tassels from the white tail tips of the bilby (a rabbitlike creature).

## Significant colors

The colors red, black, and yellow have become associated with the Aboriginal people and are used for their flag. Many indigenous people today wear headbands or jewelry in these colors or have red, black, and yellow tattoos.

###  The story of Luma Luma

The people of western Arnhem Land tell the story of how Luma Luma—their giant **ancestor spirit**—taught his people their body designs. Before he died, Luma Luma took a stone knife and cut a fine pattern of crisscrossed lines into his chest, explaining that each segment represented an area of his **country.** He instructed his people that they must wear these designs in their ceremonies.

## Body painting

Aboriginal people decorate their bodies before taking part in important **rituals.** They paint their skin with clays and **ochers** and sometimes also apply downy feathers using tree sap. Often, the patterns painted on a man's body represent the country of his society, showing in symbolic form its rocks, rivers, trees, and watering holes.

These Aboriginal boys are wearing body paint and ornaments. They are ready for an **initiation ceremony.**

# Ceremonies, Songs, and Dance

Ceremonies and **rituals** are a vital part of Aboriginal life. They combine music, dance, song, and storytelling, as well as other forms of artistic expression such as **ground art**, sculpture, and body art.

## Remembering the Dreamtime

Many Aboriginal ceremonies reenact journeys and events from the **Dreamtime**, following in the tracks of the **ancestor spirits**. Lengthy cycles of songs are performed at particular stopping points where a spirit created a feature of the landscape or a plant or animal. Ceremonies are held to release the ancestor's life-giving power.

Performers reenact the ancestors' actions, painting their skin and masking themselves with elaborate headdresses and ceremonial dress so that they take on the ancestors' identities. In the excitement of the ceremony, the presence of the ancestors can be felt by the performers.

## Initiation rituals

Some **indigenous societies** perform elaborate **initiation ceremonies** to welcome young men into their group. When a boy reaches **puberty**, he is removed from his family to spend some time in the company of men. During this time, many secret rituals are carried out by the group's **elders**.

In Arnhem Land, in northern Australia, most of the initiation rituals take place on a special ground that is screened off from the rest of the community. The women of the boy's family gather around the edge of the ground to dance and sing, **mourning** the loss of their child. At one stage in the ritual, the women charge the men with spears in a symbolic gesture of anger because their child has been taken away from them.

## Mortuary ceremonies

Another major ritual is the **mortuary ceremony**, which is intended to guide the souls of the dead back to the spirit world. In the mortuary ceremony of the Tiwi people from the Melville and Bathurst islands, songs and dances are performed around specially carved and painted posts representing dead members of a society. At the climax of the ceremony, special bark baskets are broken over the posts, symbolizing the setting free of the spirits of the dead.

## Other ceremonies

Different aspects of Aboriginal life are reflected in their ceremonies. Rain ceremonies are performed to encourage rain to fall in times of drought. Courtship rituals can involve groups of men or women performing dances and songs to suitable partners. Fire ceremonies are used to express anger or resolve a conflict. The fire ceremony symbolizes first the bringing of a grievance into the open and then the solving of that grievance by the dramatic burning of branches.

These Aboriginal dancers are preparing for a ceremony to honor the Cadigal society, the original people of the land that is now Sydney. Public ceremonies like these contain elements of the more secret rituals practiced by Aboriginal societies.

## The Morning Star ceremony

One of the most striking and complex Aboriginal rituals is the Morning Star ceremony, performed in Arnhem Land in northern Australia. This mortuary ceremony **commemorates** the journey of the Morning Star as it travels through the sky. It also traces the journey that a person's spirit must take after death. At the climax of the ceremony, performers create poles decorated with feathers and hung with tassels. The tassels are of different lengths, symbolizing different family groups. The Morning Star ceremony also illustrates the way that different groups come together to perform rituals and to trade.

## Contemporary dance

In 1989 the Bangarra Dance Theatre was founded. It aims to present **indigenous** dance traditions in a contemporary, exciting way. The company has performed all over the world. One of its best known dances, *Praying Mantis Dreaming*, is a full-length ballet inspired by a traditional dance from Arnhem Land.

*Didgeridoo* is a Westernized version of this instrument's proper name, which is the Muhggool.

### ◈ Contemporary music

During the 1980s Aboriginal musicians began to form rock bands that merged **indigenous** rhythms and sounds (such as the didgeridoo) with Western rock. Most of these bands sing about Aboriginal political themes. The most successful Aboriginal rock band is Yothu Yindi from northeastern Arnhem Land. Its early 1990s song, *"Treaty,"* was the first indigenous rock song to hit the top of the charts.

## Musical instruments

Aboriginal songs and dances are accompanied by rhythmical music made on a range of traditional instruments, such as **didgeridoos** and clapsticks. Didgeridoos are made from hollowed-out branches or tree trunks and are blown to produce loud, deep notes. Clapsticks are pairs of solid hardwood sticks that are knocked together rhythmically. Paired **boomerangs** are also often used as **percussion instruments**. Many Aboriginal instruments are painted with traditional designs and stories that add an extra layer of significance to the music.

## *Corroborees*

As early as the 1840s, European settlers in Australia showed an interest in Aboriginal ceremonies. However, the Aboriginal people wanted to keep their rituals secret, so they created special performances to entertain the settlers. In these dramatic shows, Aboriginals wore ceremonial dress and acted out a sequence of mimes, dances, and songs based on the **Dreamtime** legends. The Europeans called all the performances *corroborees*—a word taken from the Dharug language that means "a general entertainment and celebration." In fact, each Aboriginal **society** has its own name for its performances.

This early *corroboree* was painted by Samuel Thomas Gill in 1874.

# Baskets and Fiber Art

All **indigenous** Australians have a tradition of making baskets and other **fiber** works, and each region has its own materials and techniques. The finished objects may be used for storing and carrying food, trapping animals, or carrying babies. However, the baskets and other objects are also believed to be sacred and play an important part in ceremonies.

## Fiber objects from Arnhem Land

The women of northern Arnhem Land, in northern Australia, make a range of objects from plant fibers, using techniques of coiling, twining, and looping. The objects vary from large, flat mats to small coiled earrings. The most popular forms are coiled baskets that can stand unsupported and triangular carrying baskets known as **dilly bags.**

The fiber forms of Arnhem Land are closely associated with their **ancestor spirits**—especially the Djang'kawu Sisters. According to Aboriginal beliefs, the sisters carried a variety of sacred objects on their journeys, including conical mats and dilly bags, and sometimes gave birth to children by drawing them out of their mats and bags. The present-day versions of these ancestral objects have everyday uses (dilly bags are often used for collecting honey) but they are also used in ceremonies.

This dilly bag from Arnhem Land is made from plant fibers dyed with natural **pigments.** Dilly bags were essential for the plant-gathering way of life and are still used today as carrying bags.

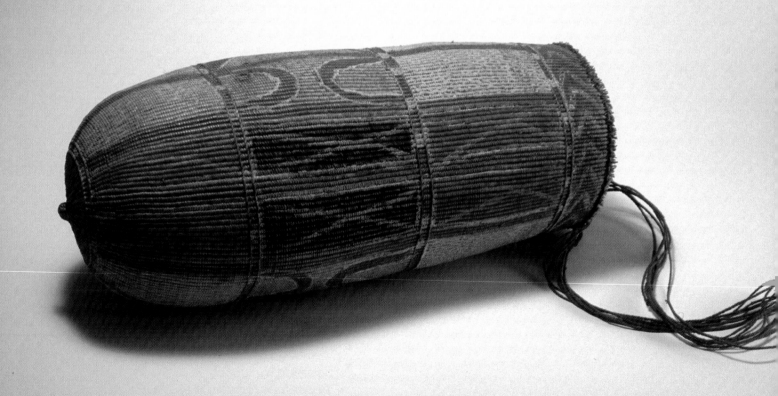

Contemporary Aboriginal artists working in Arnhem Land have taken the traditional forms in some interesting directions. Robyn Djunginy makes three-dimensional bottle forms, associated with the Honey Bee Ancestor, while Lena Yarinkura creates woven Mermaid Spirits with vividly decorated tails.

## Baskets and blankets from Queensland

In the rain forest of northern Queensland, women make crescent-shaped, two-cornered baskets from split cane. Undecorated forms of the basket are used for fishing, holding food, and even carrying children. Painted baskets have several **ritual** uses. The baskets are usually painted in red, yellow, and white, and can be used to carry **ceremonial objects,** to offer trading objects to members of another **society,** or to present a gift to a friend.

Until the early 20th century, the rain forest people hammered the inner bark of fig trees to made soft bark blankets, but these have now been replaced by woolen blankets.

## Eel traps and baskets from the southeast

In some areas of southeast Australia, the Ngarrindjeri people make coiled baskets that are used as eel traps, fish scoops, gathering baskets, and weapon holders. These traditional forms have been adapted by some contemporary artists. As early as the 1920s, Janet Watson used the coiling technique to create models of planes. Yvonne Koolmatrie produces semiabstract sculptures based on the shapes of conical eel traps.

This Aboriginal woman is dyeing fiber from the pandanus tree. It will be used to make mats and baskets.

# Other Media

By the late 20th century, increased contact with other cultures meant that **indigenous** artists had begun to try out a range of new forms and materials, such as ceramics and **batiks**. Other types of art, such as poster making and car door painting, are used by Aboriginal artists to convey political messages.

## Pottery

Aboriginal people do not traditionally make pots, but in the early 1990s a group of artists at Hermannsburg, near Alice Springs, began experimenting with ceramic forms. The Hermannsburg potters produce hand-built round pots with small **figurines** molded on to their lids. The pots are painted with colorful scenes that owe their original inspiration to the watercolor paintings of the Hermannsburg artist Albert Namatjira. The first pots featured Australian landscapes and creatures, but recently the Hermannsburg potters have introduced a range of non-Australian subjects, such as zebras and tigers.

## Utopia batiks

During the 1970s, the Aboriginal women of Utopia, in the central desert region, became well known for their batiks. These are designs on fabric made by covering parts of the cloth in wax during the dyeing process.

The Utopia batiks were very colorful. They contained repeated patterns, often featuring flower **motifs.** Utopia batiks relate traditional stories from the **Dreamtime** and many of them look similar to Western Desert paintings.

This silk batik from Utopia features a floral design. Utopia batiks are known for their lively patterns and vivid colors.

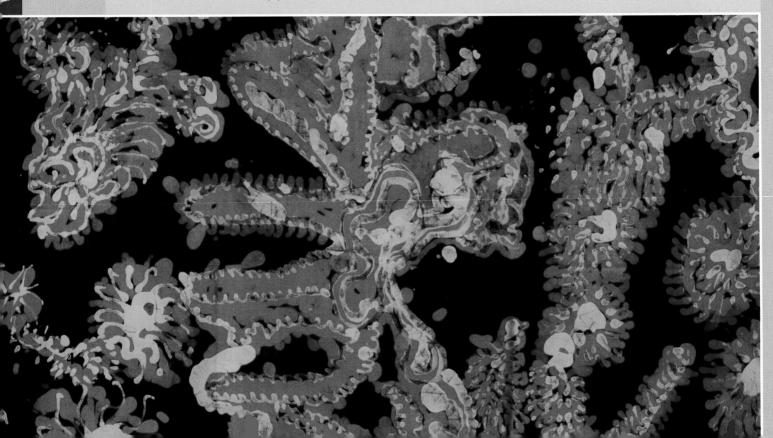

A spectacular mosaic forms the courtyard of the new **Parliament** House in Canberra. Designed by the Western Desert artist Michael Nelson Tjakamarra, it is a large-scale image of a Dreamtime journey.

## Painted car doors

One recent form of indigenous art is the painted car door. Artists such as Mavis Holmes decorate car doors with traditional Aboriginal designs using vivid **acrylic paints.** The images form a poignant comment on the clash of ancient and modern cultures. The painted cars also express their artists' contradictory attitudes to the car, which destroys the traditional culture of following the **dreaming tracks,** but allows far greater contact between the scattered Aboriginal peoples.

## Posters

From the 1970s onward, groups of Aboriginals formed **collectives** to make posters. The bold, attention-getting posters had a political message, raising awareness of land rights and encouraging a sense of pride in Aboriginal history.

## Writing and film

Storytelling is very important in Aboriginal culture, but until recently the Aboriginal people had not produced a large number of written works. In the 1960s two indigenous poets, Colin Johnson (Mudrooroo) and Kath Walker (Oodgeroo), began to write about the Aboriginal experience. Twenty years later, the playwright Jack Davis wrote a series of powerful plays about the tensions between Aboriginals and white communities. His most famous play is *No Sugar* (1985).

Recently, Aboriginal writers have started producing novels, short stories, and true life stories. Indigenous filmmakers such as Tracey Moffatt and Rachel Perkins have written and directed full-length feature films about contemporary Aboriginal life, but very few of these films have been publicly released.

# Crosscurrents

When early settlers first discovered examples of Aboriginal art, they dismissed them as primitive and uninteresting. Most Aboriginal paintings were described as "crude" or "rough," while any particularly skillful examples were believed to have been influenced by European art. This attitude remained basically unchanged throughout the 19th century, but by the 1920s some Europeans were beginning to appreciate **indigenous** Australian art.

In her striking **lithoprint** *Tea Tree Blossoms,* Margaret Preston imitated the decorative techniques used in Aboriginal art.

## Changing attitudes

In the early 20th century, the **anthropologist** Baldwin Spencer collected examples of art from all over Australia, and in 1929 he held the first major Australian Aboriginal art exhibition in Melbourne. Other exhibitions followed, and by the 1980s all the major museums and galleries in Australia had large collections of indigenous art. Since then, Australian museums and galleries have continued to collect and display both traditional art and pieces by contemporary indigenous artists. There is a thriving market in Aboriginal art and many practicing artists are supported by government-sponsored grants.

## Aboriginal influence

Although attitudes about Aboriginal art slowly changed in the early 20th century, indigenous art had very little impact on other artists working in Australia. However, one exception was Margaret Preston (1875–1963). Preston wanted to create a distinctively Australian style and sought inspiration from Aboriginal art. She visited central Australia and western Arnhem Land, where she was struck by the artists' bold depiction of animal and plant forms and. She also admired their strong use of outline and decorative patterns. She incorporated these elements into her paintings.

*Blue Haze over James Range* is a painting by Albert Namatjira. In Namatjira's works, the light is stronger and the shapes are starker than in European landscapes of the same period.

## European influence

While most indigenous artists continued to follow their ancient traditions until the 1970s, a few early 20th-century artists were influenced by European styles. The most famous example of this occurred in the 1930s at Hermannsburg in central Australia. Here, a painter named Rex Battarbee taught an Aboriginal artist, Albert Namatjira (1902–1959), to paint landscapes in the European style. Namatjira became extremely famous. He produced pencil drawings and watercolors and also decorated **boomerangs** and spear throwers with his painted landscapes. Other Aboriginal painters also adopted a European style, and the Hermannsburg School flourished until the 1950s.

## A different vision

Although Albert Namatjira followed the European watercolor tradition, his paintings look very different from landscapes produced by non-Aboriginal artists of the period. His landscapes are empty of any sign of human life and there is a sense of delight in the bold shapes and colors of the trees and mountains. This vision affected later non-Aboriginal artists who tried to abandon their European viewpoints and paint the Australian landscape with fresh eyes.

## A new generation

In the late 1970s a new generation of **indigenous** artists began to emerge from the art schools of Australia. These artists were trained in European techniques, styles, and materials, but also drew on traditional subjects and **motifs** to create works with a powerful political message.

This new generation of artists lives mainly in the cities of the southeast. They are sometimes known as urban Aboriginal artists.

## Art with a message

Aboriginal artists today work in a wide range of media. They produce works that reflect their people's past and comment on their place in modern society.

Harry J. Wedge and Robert Campbell Junior paint scenes such as the arrival of Captain Cook, the early massacres of the Aboriginal people, and their people's fight for equal rights. Both painters' work is arresting, vivid, and includes strong traditional elements. Wedge features boldly outlined figures and Campbell uses tiny dots to build up a highly patterned surface.

Trevor Nickolls produces detailed paintings that vividly contrast the natural world of the Aboriginal people with ugly cities and mines. Gordon Bennett draws on elements from European art to comment on Aboriginal life. For example, Bennett's painting *Outsider* is a version of Vincent van Gogh's *Bedroom at Arles*. It features a decapitated Aboriginal figure who spurts blood all over the room.

A major figure in contemporary Aboriginal art was Lin Onus, who died in 1996. Onus worked in a range of media to make his powerful and witty statements about the impact of the Western world on the Aboriginal way of life. One of his most famous works, *Fruit Bats*, features a colony of beautifully carved and painted wooden bats hanging upside-down from a washing line.

Like Lin Onus, Fiona Foley makes challenging sculptures from carved objects. Sally Morgan creates striking prints with a clear political message. In her print *Another Story*, the land underneath an idyllic farm building is revealed to be full of Aboriginal victims' bodies.

## A new approach

In the 21st century, one of the world's most ancient artistic traditions is being given new life. Museums and galleries throughout the world exhibit traditional examples of Aboriginal art, while contemporary indigenous artists play an important role in the international art scene.

With its bright primary colors and deceptively simple composition, Sally Morgan's *Taken Away* (1987) appears at first glance to be a cheerful picture, but its subject is a dark one. It shows the fate of the stolen generation—children who were forcibly removed from their Aboriginal mothers and brought up by white people. Morgan's picture is a protest against this cruel practice, which lasted from the 1890s to the 1960s.

# Further Resources

## Further reading

Alter, Judy. *Discovering Australia's Land, People, and Wildlife.* Berkeley Heights, N.J.: Enslow Publishers, 2004.

Arnold, Caroline. *Uluru: Australia's Aboriginal Heart.* Boston: Houghton Mifflin, 2003.

Bartlett, Anne. *The Aboriginal Peoples of Australia.* Minneapolis: Lerner Publishing, 2001.

Caruana, Wally. *Aboriginal Art.* New York: Thames and Hudson, 2003.

Cobb, Leigh Ann. *Australia.* Chicago: Raintree, 2002.

Einfeld, Jann. *Life in the Australian Outback.* Farmington Hills, Mich.: Gale Group, 2002.

Finley, Carol. *Aboriginal Art of Australia: Exploring Cultural Traditions.* Minneapolis, Minn.: Lerner Publishing, 1998.

Marshall, Diana. *Aboriginal Australians.* New York: Weigl Publishers, 2004.

Richardson, Margot. *Australia.* Chicago: Raintree, 2003.

## Using the Internet

Explore the Internet to find out more about Aboriginal art and culture. Have an adult help you use a search engine. Type in a keyword, such as *Dreamtime, X-ray painting,* or *Uluru.*

## Places to visit

Dreamtime Gallery, Sante Fe, New Mexico

Long Beach Museum of Art, California

Lowe Art Museum, University of Miami, Florida

Pacific Asia Museum, Los Angeles, California

Peabody Museum of Natural History, Yale University, New Haven, Connecticut

# Glossary

**acrylic paint** paint made from chemicals rather than natural dyes. Acrylic paints are often very bright.

**amenity** service, such as running water, that makes life comfortable

**ancestor spirits** spirits who created the world in the Dreamtime and who live on in landscape features, animals, and plants and in the memories and art of the Aboriginal people

**anthropologist** someone who studies the way people live or lived

**batik** method of coloring fabric in which parts of the fabric are covered with wax before the fabric is dyed

**binder** substance used to make things bind or stick together

**boomerang** curved, flat piece of wood that is thrown into the air and then returns to the thrower. Boomerangs are used for hunting animals and birds.

**boomerang club** wooden club, used for hunting

**ceremonial ground** place where ceremonies are held

**ceremonial object** sacred object, such as a carving, used in ceremonies

**collective** group of people who work together to produce something

**colony** settlement created in a foreign land by a group of people who have moved away from their homeland

**commemorate** remember with respect

**convict** someone who has been found guilty of a crime

**cooperative** group of people who work together to make something

**country** word used by Aboriginal people to describe the area of land for which they were responsible

**crosshatched** marked with sets of parallel lines crossing each other

**didgeridoo** Aboriginal wind instrument made from a hollowed-out branch or tree trunk

**dilly bag** small bag, often made from plaited grass, used for carrying food

**dingo** wild Australian dog with a bushy tail and reddish-brown hair

**dreaming tracks** tracks made by the ancestor spirits in their journeys across Australia during the Dreamtime

**Dreamtime** according to Aboriginal beliefs, the time when the world was created

**elder** older member of a community, seen as wiser and more experienced than others

**emu** large, flightless bird found in Australia

**engraving** carving on a rock or any another hard surface

**eucalyptus** type of tree that grows in many parts of Australia. Eucalyptus trees often have a papery bark and their leaves produce a strong-smelling oil.

**fiber** threads from plants or animal hair that can be woven into cloth or other items

**figurine** small carved or molded figure

**ground art** art that is drawn on the earth, or that is made from shaping earth

**Ice Age** period in the history of Earth, when large areas were covered by sheets of ice. The last Ice Age lasted from about 100,000 to 10,000 years ago.

**indigenous** belonging to a place

**initiation ceremony** ceremony held for young people to mark their coming of age and to welcome them as adult members of society

**lithoprint** print made by using a metal plate with a design cut into it

**memorial** something created to honor the memory of the dead

**missionary** person sent on a religious mission

**mortuary ceremony** ceremony held to honor the dead

**motif** design or pattern

**mourning** practice of remembering and honoring the dead

**ocher** earth. Ocher paints are made from earth.

**parliament** name for the legislative body in some countries, similar to Congress in the United States

**penal colony** place to which convicted criminals are taken where they have to live and work together

**percussion instrument** musical instrument that is struck or shaken to make a noise

**pigment** paint or dye, usually made from natural materials

**pokerwork** designs made by burning a wooden surface with a hot metal object, such as a needle or a poker

**populated** filled with people

**puberty** time when a young person's body changes, as the child becomes an adult

**reservation** area of land that is set aside for native people to live on. In Australia reservations are known as reserves.

**ritual** traditional actions and ceremonies, used to mark special occasions

**rock painting** painting on rocks and cliffs

**sacred site** place that is associated with an ancestor spirit

**settlement** place where people have settled down in groups to live

**society** group of people who are related to each other, share the same traditions, and live in the same area

**status** position in society

**stencil** shape filled in with colored paint

**stylized** exaggerated and slightly abstract

**termite** antlike insect that feeds on wood

# Index